# Earth Carries Spirit

AF471918

# Earth Carries Spirit

Poems By
Thelma Ann Brennan

Chapel Street Editions
Woodstock, New Brunswick

Copyright © 2014 Thelma Ann Brennan
All rights reserved.

Published by Chapel Street Editions,
Woodstock, NB, Canada
www.chapelstreeteditions.com

Library and Archives Canada Cataloguing in Publication

Brennan, Thelma Ann, author

Earth carries spirit : poems by Thelman Ann Brennan.

ISBN 978-0-9936725-2-4 (pbk.)

I. Title.

CIP data available from Library and Archives Canada

Designed by Helmuth Productions using Adobe® InDesign.®
The typeface used is Averia Serif. Designed by Dan Sayer.
http://iotic.com/averia/

Portrait of the author on the back cover by Shirley Bear, 1988

The triple spiral, or triskele shown on the cover, is a Celtic and pre-Celtic symbol found on a number of Irish Megalithic and Neolithic sites, most notably inside the Newgrange passage tomb, on the entrance stone, and on some of the curbstones surrounding the mound. A wide range of meanings are associated with the triskele, including life, death, and rebirth; land, sky, and sea; maiden, mother, crone (Earth Goddess). The triple spiral has been widely used in Celtic art for over three millennia and became incorporated in the art of Celtic Christianity.

*James Miley's Pub* previously published in Canadian Women's Studies: Women of Ireland, Summer/Fall 1997, Vol. 17, Number 3.

*Shared Beginnings* previously published in Vox Feminarum: The Canadian Journal of Feminist Spirituality, Fall/Winter 1998, Volume 2, Issue 2.

*Journey Home* previously published in Stories in *My Neighbor's Faith: Narratives from World Religions in Canada*. Edited by Susan L. Scott: United Church Publishing House: Toronto, Canada, 1999.

# Contents

# Acknowledgments

I wish to thank Keith and Ellen Helmuth for their guidance, patience and the courage to create Chapel Street Editions. Special thanks to Brendan Helmuth for his creativity, and technical skill in designing and producing this book.

Thank you to my special friend Elizabeth Dawn Lockwood for insisting that I write this book and to my family for their unwavering support.

Finally, I wish to express my love and dedicate this book to the readers of these poems and hope you believe, as I do, that poetry can change the world.

## Foreword

*Earth Carries Spirit* is more than a collection of poems: It is a cultural document that reaches deeply into the heritage of the human-earth relationship and forward into the future of people and planet. This double movement is accomplished by Ann Brennan's poetic portrayal of her experiences across a panorama of time and place. The lens is personal, but the perspective is inclusive: It brings in the spirituality of earth in human experience, the restoration of earth's ecological integrity, and the kind of healing for both people and the earth that is needed for a culture of peace and wellbeing.

Ann Brennan lives and writes in a tradition of perception and expression that has deep roots in the poetic vocation. Things come to her and she responds. She then prepares herself for what may come next. She says, "I'm just the writer." But as a writer she stands in a long tradition of aesthetic and spiritual response to knowledge, experience, and wisdom.

Ezra Pound observed in *ABC of Reading* (1934) that "artists are the antenna of the race." In the 1960s, Marshall McLuhan extended this metaphor into a discussion of how artists serve as "an early warning system" for the trajectories of cultural change.

The sense that poets are sometimes instruments of revelatory wisdom emerges with particular force in William Blake. He looked into the heart of things and countered the energy of "the dark satanic mills" with the vision of a "New Jerusalem" built "in England's green and pleasant land." William Wordsworth, likewise, drew up his "unmediated vision" into poetic expression:

*While with an eye made quiet by the power*
*Of harmony, and the deep power of joy,*
*We see into the life of things.*

Percy Bysshe Shelley declared that, "Poets are the unacknowledged legislators of the world."

Some may think Shelley exaggerates, but this proclamation, along with Blake's prayer - "May God keep us from Single Vision and Newton's sleep" - still fly like banners of courage over the restoration of the poetic vocation. Ann Brennan's poetry, as collected in *Earth Carries Spirit*, is yet another flag raised on the field of this restoration. A growing number of poets now understand their vocation entails an engagement with the spirituality of earth, and, indeed with a defence of earth and the unity of its whole community of life.

Although composed of four sections, each with poems of several kinds, *Earth Carries Spirit* achieves an unmistakable unity. The motif of the journey develops as a double movement, a movement that is both an inward quest to connect with the spirituality of earth, and an outward engagement with people, culture, and the realities of various environments.

The book begins with "Going Home to Ireland," a section in which the quintessential double movement develops in high relief. On the one hand the author's journey is a personal quest for a vital connection with the land and culture of her ancestors. But it is also, simultaneously, an engagement with the people she encounters and the contemporary realities of Ireland, including, and especially, the Irish Peace Process.

"Circles of Time and Place" widens the perspective both temporally and geographically, including travels to Estonia and to the Ukraine at the time of the Orange Revolution where the author was an official Canadian election observer. As this section flows from her experience in Ireland, it becomes clear the author's poetic vocation is inscribed with a "calling" – a calling to help bring healing to a badly wounded earth and to the distress of people suffering deep divisions.

"In Dreams Begin the Courage of the Spirit" speaks with acute awareness of life's double movement. A poetic vocation that includes this kind of calling can only unfold in the courage of the spirit, and the courage of the spirit arises from the strength and integrity of dreams – both those that visit us and those we nurture into reality. "Seasons of Words on the Edge of Silence" brings together poems that contrast images of fullness and emptiness, contentment and conflict, along with reflections on the poetic vocation that is moved to hold it all in balance.

*Earth Carries Spirit* is a journey, a journey that gives voice to Ann Brennan's blended vocation of poet and healer. A book like this is highly personal and requires courage to compose and share. Once shared, however, it becomes a cultural treasure and an ongoing guide to the healing transformation of both the earth and the human world.

*Keith Helmuth*

# Going Home to Ireland

# Prelude

In the beginning our ancestors carried soil from place to place when they traveled. They believed they were part of the earth and the soil carried its spirit. When the emigrants left their homeland, mothers wrapped small parcels of soil in a towel hoping to carry that spirit with them. As I began my spiritual journey I intuitively carried soil in a small medicine bundle not realizing that I too was repeating the pattern of those who went before me.

*Earth Carries Spirit* is a collection of poems that symbolize that same belief in the oneness of the universe and that the soil connects us to the spirit of the land. When I first returned to the place of my ancestors I was overwhelmed by the feelings and longings of the land. The land drew me in like a magnet. Words came with ease as I found my spiritual attachment to the earth.

I was compelled to learn the stories, histories and legends so I could fully understand these deep feelings and emotions I could only express in poetry. I began to study the heroic tales of Cú Chulainn, hero of the Tain, Manannan Mac Lir, God of the Sea and of the Tuatha Dé Dannan, the mysterious tribe who once inhabited the land of my ancestors. In legend, story, and song, I began to discover secrets of the earth that I had never imagined.

Listening to my heart when I travel to a new country, I introduce myself to the spirit of the land scattering bits of earth and sage so that the spirits will recognize my respect for the earth.

Come travel with me now through the cities, towns and little villages, over the hills to Slieve Foy the legendary home of the leprechauns and down into the valley where the fairies are known to dwell. The journey is sweet, the air is pure and the spirit of magick abounds.

*The Farm*
*Johnville, New Brunswick*
*August 24, 2014*

# Old Wives' Tale

One crow sorrow
Two crows joy
Three crows a letter...

My friend lives in the woods nearby
We have a silent understanding he and I
Like the good friend he truly is
He does not come often
But when he comes alone
I am prepared for sadness
Yesterday, as I gathered the mail
He came accompanied by two friends
They laughed at me and flew away

There was a letter from Aunt Phyllis
And the money for the trip to Ireland

*Johnville, New Brunswick*
*September, 1987*

## Going Home

Going back in time
On Aer Lingus
We faced a fuchsia sunrise
Entered a time warp over the ocean
Anticipated the Singing Stone and Cú Chulainn
Red-haired Irish boys and love

*Over the Atlantic Ocean*
*Nearing Shannon*

## Inishowen

My friends write poetry for me
I am touched by the brilliance of their words
Moved by their love
Humbled by their friendship
I have been fortunate to have
Passed through this life
Surrounded by the great ones
Roy, an Irish Bard filled with sorrow and greatness
Shirley, my sweat keeper
My Medicine Woman
Antagonist and friend
Always pushing me to greater heights
The children all
Children of my body
Children of my soul
Surround me with gifts
Gifts of words and poetry
Lawrence, who will continue the eagle's search
Rayanne, who will write my dreams
Neil, who will lead us all
Pam, who will be my rock
Together the children will hold and sway
To the rhythm of the drum
Holding the dream
That brought us all together
To witness magic in Inishowen

## Hillside Ramblings

Earth and stone
Earth and bones
Ireland, Ireland
It is to you I return

Open arms
And open heart
From your shores
May I never part

Earth and stone
Earth and bones
Turf and fire
Flute and lyre

Song of Scota
Stories of a traveling Bard
On these ancient cliffs
May I retire

Earth and stone
Earth and bones
Sands of time
Do make the rhyme

Castles, hills and battlements
Cover the land
In the footsteps of my ancestors
I will stand

## Grainan of Aileach

The heart beats
The heart beats

The earth speaks
The earth speaks

The drum beats
The drum beats

And I dream
And I dream

And I fly
And I fly

And I listen
And I listen

I hear whispers
I hear whispers

The stones speak
The stones speak

I remember
I remember

Talisen, Talisen
Amergin, Amergin

Calling, calling
My heart beats

And I wait
And I wait

The stones speak
The stones speak

*Inishowen*
*County Donegal*

## If Stones Could Speak

If stones could speak
And I could truly fly
The world would be a better place
For all who dream
But stones do speak
And stones don't lie
They tell their stories
Of days gone by
They stand and watch
The passers-by
And hold their secrets
For you and I

Poets, dreamers
Children too
Watch and wait, anticipate
The stories of the days of old
Of ladies fair
And warriors bold
Castle walls and carrion cries

The stones do hold their secrets well
There are those who will not tell
Though they know where secrets dwell
Some see the spirits in the night
Know the special places in the glen
Hidden caves and secret dens
Remain untouched for ages past
Waiting for the call at last
To free the land from frozen time
When a Druid comes to complete this rhyme

# Love at First Sight

Dublin, fair city
You were dressed in black
The first time we met
Heavy with grayness, drabness
Dreariness, weariness and sadness
Air, filled with stone dust
Yet you reflected the dichotomy of Ireland
With gay store fronts
Brilliant with their shining wood
And polished brass
They showed a bravery of spirit
The men of your streets
Dressed in their seedy, tweedy jackets
Adjusted their jaunty caps
As they proceeded
To saunter off to the pub
They walked with a swagger
As they wait for Brian the Brave
And the call to Clontarf

## Beginnings

Our dreams are no longer
The same as our forefathers
Yet we must make the journey
In search of our beginnings
We dig the earth
In a strange land
Gathering fragments
Carry them back
So that on winter nights
We can reminisce
Remembering the hills
And Celtic crosses
We convince ourselves
We are better off than Tommy Brynes
Who goes to Lisdoonvarna
Match Making Festival
To find himself a wife

*Lisdoonvarna*
*County Clare*

# Baptism at Ennis

The young mother beams with pride
The man beside her shifts his feet
Embarrassed that his passion
Has taken a visible form
The priest sprinkles holy water
Rubs oil on the forehead
Of the sleeping infant
Muffled voices echo
Through the hollow cathedral
Brilliant Sunday light
Shines through stained glass
"Bless this child and give him hope."
The priest places salt upon his lips
Ah, the bitter with the sweet
Another soul for Ireland
A future bricklayer for Boston

*Ennis*
*County Clare*

## Kathleen O'Meara Colfer

Sitting on the pump stand
Among the brambles
They remember the thirties
And the Land Commission
Sisters crying together
At the ancient rites and symbols
All gone and past now
Tears follow fears
Fears follow emptiness
Earth and silt covers the land
As Kathleen O'Meara Colfer
And her sisters
Sit and sing
Among the brambles
All united by the unseen spirits
Of the Tuatha Dé Danaan

*Cullenstown*
*County Wexford*

## Cousins

There were tears in your eyes
When I left Mary Sorohan
I thought it strange
As we had just met
I was a stranger from away
A Canadian with an accent
A woman who had borne children like you
We had the same large feet and thin hair
Even though our meeting was brief
We are united forever Mary Sorohan
Joined by the knowledge
That far away in Canada
Lives a woman who shares a name
And a thatched cottage in Greenore

*Dublin*

## Carrickmacross

"There is a knock at the door."
"Let them in!"
"It's an American cousin."
"Keep him out!"
"Let him in!"
"He'll wave the flag
Of freedom
For there is work in New York
But none for us here
In Carrickmacross."

"There is a knock at the door."
"Let them in!"
"It's an American cousin
With a bottle of gin!"
"Let him in."
"Keep him out
For he will steal all our children
And take them away
To dig in their ditches
And build their fine bridges
Never again to return
To Carrickmacross."

"There is a knock at the door."
"Let them in!"
"It's our Canadian cousin
He's here for the war
Wanted to stop
And give us full heart

They are doing their best
On that far distant shore
The trees are so grand there
And the hills never end there
There's work for us all there
If only we'd leave
Our dear Carrickmacross"

"There's a knock at the door."
"Let them in!"
"But it's the devil himself
With a world full of sin!"
"Keep him out."
"Let him in
For there's nothing
For us here
In Carrickmacross."

"Sure the magpies are laughing
And the hillside is green
But there's no need explaining
To the babes in the crib
There's more to the living
Then ballads and sea
We need to go forward
To change the whole world."

"There's a knock at the door."
"Let them in!"

*Carrickmacross*
*County Monaghan*

# Tribute to Fergus Grant

Dear Fergie
Descendent of an ancient tribe
Just now fitting in between
The high babies and the low

Child with the ability to speak
In the Celtic tongue of our ancestors
Stand in front of strangers
And recite poetry without hesitation

You are indeed a precocious child
With dancing eyes
And impish grin
Always able to steal your Mother's heart

You want a poem and a Quest
Every boy needs a Quest
Since I am a writer
I can decree any Quest I so desire

For you dear Fergie
Your task of youth will be
To go to the mountains
And find the ancient castle of Dun Dealgan

Dig deep beneath the ruins
And watch for ravens overhead
When you discover the ancient truths
Then you will understand
The meaning of poetry

*Dundalk*
*County Louth*

# Limerick

City blocks and city streets
Enclose my mind and heart
Wrought iron railings
And stone walls
Make a prisoner of my heart

Not even magpies or rose bushes
Can make me smile
I need room to spread and dance
Feel the wind blowing through the trees

I can never again be a city child
Play hopscotch or roller skate
I need earth and pine needles
Beneath my feet

*County Limerick*

## The Shell House

On the edge of sea and sky
Kevin Ffrench made a house of shells
Reminiscent of a fairy tale
He sits outside and taunts the passer-by
"If you think this place is so special,
It will cost you £5 to take a picture."

He shouts obscenities
And slams his door
Inside his house
His wife calls him up for tea
While in his mind Kevin plans
The next side to his masterpiece

With sharp edged trowel
He places intricate shells
In perfect lines and symmetry
Along the sides and on every corner of his house

He scowls at the brave tourist
Who dares to venture near
While behind him his mosaic art
Glistens and shines against the sky
Reflecting peace and love
On the waters of Bannow Bay

*Cullenstown*
*County Wexford*

# Charity, Sweet Charity

I am still having trouble
Leaving my guilt on the Halfpenny Bridge
The ugly girl who cradled a pathetic infant
Begged for money with a dirty plastic dish
Mary Sorohan told me to walk past
The girl would only use the money
To buy cheap wine, she scoffed
Who am I to come to Dublin and offer judgment
On the crowds who choose to ignore her
So I walked on, pulled my purse tight
Carrying my guilt in my heart
Wondering what Jesus would have done
Were he a tourist on the Halfpenny Bridge

*Dublin*

## Belfast Docks

It seems ironic
That ships are referred to as maidens
Yet it is always men
Who build them

In the Belfast docks
It was men who launched her
On to the ocean brave
It is they who watched
Her sail away

Yet it was they who offered no claim
When the Titanic sank in shame
They showed no ownership
For the maiden
Who lies buried on the ocean floor

# James Miley's Pub

The dancing spirits are not here
In James Miley's pub
Glass globes are sparkling clean
Antlers and a ram's head hang over the bar
Liquor bottles are placed carefully in line
The fireplace burns real wood
Not the poor Catholic's dirty coal
Windows reflect expensive panes of bubble glass
The prestigious doorknocker is polished brass
We never expect a guffaw from James Miley
Not in fifty years of trade
How boring, how dull,
Oh hell! Oh well!
We can always go to McCarthy's next door

*Blessington*
*County Wicklow*

## Ghosts by the Sea

Vines and bracken cover the stones
Creeping up the ancient walls
Walls built by men long ago
Walls that are adorned with cherubs
Stone heads of angels, saints and sinners
They watch over us as we walk through the mist
In the distance we hear
The sea break against the shore
Washing away the traces
Of those who have walked before
Men chanting their mantras
In rhyme with the sea
Sounds hang on the trees
Trees that remember
Constant chant
Rhythm and rhyme
Earth and stone
Sea and time
United in the ebb and flow
The Abbey beckons us to enter

*Tintern Abbey, Hook Pennisula*
*County Wexford*

# Slieve Foy

At the wishing well
I pause and wait
For I do not know
What the wish should be
So wishes spent
And wishes lent
Do not answer
The question meant
What is in my heart
Which I truly do require
Happiness and health
Eternity or wealth?

I have them all
Within my grasp
The well beside me
Grants all three
But yet, I pause
And question, eternity?

The water flows from high above
Tumbling over rock and dell
Into the earth
To reappear again

At the middle of the well
For all my questions
And all my thoughts
I cannot ask for more
Than to return again
To this very spot
The wishing well
In Slieve Foy Glen

*Carlingford*
*County Louth*

# Tribute to P. J. O'Hare

P. J. O'Hare was a man who believed in magic
He sent the children to the hills in search of gold
He himself had witnessed the other world
And brought back proof of his encounter

There in P. J.'s Pub in Carlingford, Ireland
Lay the last remains of an unnamed Sprite
A glass case gently enfolds the wee small bones
And tiny green suit, neat as you please

To those doubters and skeptics who come from away
And scoff and twitter in the presence of magic
We'll leave them all to be
For we of the Cooley Hills
Will never doubt
A man of the stature of P. J. O'Hare
Who taught us all to believe in leprechauns

*Carlingford*
*County Louth*

## Climbing Slieve Foy

Come fly away with me
Over the hill and mountain trail
Step back into the veil of long ago
Follow the stones
That are cast against
A blue sky
They will guide your way
To the Táin
Heroes, Cú Chulainn and Maeve
Simmer beneath the earth
They will rise up
And walk with you
Briskly at first
Thorn bushes
Will try to pull
You back into reality
But keep up
Run, step
Over the mushy earth
Water runs down the mountain
Trying to escape the past
Allow your steps to immerse
Into the soft earth
You must go deep
Before you can walk free

Up over crag and heather
Within sight of Maeve's bosom
She pulls you forward
Stop, sit and listen
To the wind
To the birds who
Announce your coming
Once the journey begins
The whole earth
Becomes part of the quest

Strangers pass
On the downward slope
Theirs is a different day
They too bring light
The clouds clear
The sun appears
Warming your back
Lifting you higher and higher

Horses in the distance
Raise their heads
In acknowledgement
Of your coming
Up, up

Breathless
The top is reached
You have walked the mountain
Of the ancients
Felt them in your bones
Smelt them in the air
The four directions are visible
As you cast your eyes
Over the landscape
Mountain, hill and dale
Spread before you
Earth and sky
Touch in the distance
Your mind snaps a photo
To be tucked away in images
To be retrieved on winter nights
When you want to fly again
Up and over the mountain tops
Back to the hills of home
Land safely on the rough ground
The journey never finished
The joy has just begun

*Carlingford*
*County Louth*

# Meeting Ghosts in Guildhall

I've been to Derry to see the Mayor
Followed the staircase round Guildhall
Saw where the bombs blew Victoria off the wall
Looked at the pieces of metal and glass
Asked for our ancestors
And was told not to laugh
For the man on the stairs
Staring down at our crew
Was none other than Ellis
The Baronet of Derry in 1702

What right had he there
We questioned our guide
The right of history to follow his path
For he built the walls to protect the few
And little did he know
That the walls he would build
Would be riddled in blood

So now as we walked up the stairs
I can only dare gaze
And never admit
That I am here to repent
For the wall that he built
For you see, I am part of the past
Part of the present
And sure as I'm standing here on the stairs
I am part of his blood

Directed by his past
To come to you now
And push the wall in

I have come to where
The apprentice boys stood
And remember the battle and sacrifice here
I feel the blood stir with memories still
But don't ask me to kneel
For I am a new breed of woman
And there is no time left
For kneeling and death
Only time left
To push the wall in

*Londonderry/Derry*

# Flight of the Earls

Myth and legends tell us that at one time eagles lived and thrived in the north of Ireland and were protected by the shamans, druids and holy people. They were revered by all and considered the symbolic life force of the north. The constant battles and struggle for power in Northern Ireland climaxed on September 14, in 1607 with the exodus of the aristocracy from the shores of Inishowen.

The leading noblemen along with their families and ninety followers boarded a French boat to flee their beloved homeland to go into permanent exile in France and Spain. The departure of the ancient Gaelic aristocracy became know in history, song and poetry as The Flight of the Earls. Ironically the exile included eagles as the sacred birds disappeared at the same time from the hills and valleys. Oral traditions passed from generation to generation told that in the far distant future the return of an eagle to the north would be a sign. Their return would signify the beginning of a new era in Ulster. For centuries children were encouraged to go to the hills in search of the ancient bird as the North waited for the struggles to end and for peace to return to their homeland.

## Peace Comes to Ulster

They say there is no hope
Here in Ulster
The war will never end
The peace talks
Have broken down again
In yesterday's paper
Ian Paisley called
John Major a fool
My comrades and I
Have gathered here
At the foot of the mountain
To talk and seek some
Radical thought
To discuss history
Philosophy
But never to discuss the war
June came to me, a stranger,
And asked: "What do you think?
Will it ever end?"
And I, reluctant to enter
Someone else's war
Only smile
I dare not say
For who am I, to enter into
Someone else's story
I did not write the play
But yet: I am drawn
Like a magnet

To the scene
The mountain looms
Behind us
And I watch for signs
Signs of hope
Dorothy said she
Saw a buzzard yesterday
“A buzzard?” I ask
“Could it have been an eagle?”
We go out after
Supper to look
Searching the sky
For a glimpse of flight
But there is none
Perhaps it is hopeless
We return to Jennifer Johnston’s reading
It is depressing
A woman
Whose husband is in Long Kesh
Probably a true story
Which is more depressing

In the morning
The sky is grey
And with my companions
We are compelled
To climb the mountain
We pull ourselves
Up and over the rocks
Lungs bursting, seeking air to breathe

Not yet daring to look
At the beauty of the land
For fear it will fade before our eyes
The journey begun
We climb and climb again
My lungs fill with air
My heart pounds
With a sense of triumph
I reach the top
High, high overhead
In the distance, I see something
Could it be?
I call the others over to bear witness
Two eagles circle and make the figure
Of a mandala
Peace, unity and infinity
There is hope
For those who dare to climb mountains
On Thursday morning
Tom Moore of Newry
Speaks of our walking tour
On Radio Ulster
He tells the listeners
An eagle has been sighted
Perhaps there truly is
Hope

*John Hewitt Summer School, July 1994*
*Garron Tower*
*County Antrim, Northern Ireland*
*IRA declaration of complete ceasefire in*
*Northern Ireland announced on August 31, 1994*

## Rosaleen

Knit one,
Purl one,
Rosaleen
Weave the dreams
Of Inishowen

Knit one,
Purl one,
Put the wool tight
Rosaleen
Tie the women to each other
Bring down the borders
With your wool
Knit one,
Purl one,
Rosaleen

*Buncrana*
*County Donegal*

# August 12th The Apprentice Boys Parade

## The Relief of Londonderry 1689

Unable to leave the past behind, the City of Londonderry, Northern Ireland continues to commemorate the defeats and victories of past wars that keep the wounds of the past open. One celebration that highlights the summer's activities is August 12th celebrated each year as the Apprentice Boys Relief of the City. On that day in 1689 the English war ship broke the booms in the River Foyle thus relieving the besieged Protestant Planters who had been surrounded for months by the Catholic troops of King James.

Nowhere is the re-enactment of history more hotly debated than in the bars of the city the night preceding the parade. On August 12th, each year, half of the city's population leave their homes to go for a drive in the country to get away from a past that is best forgotten, while the other half march to perpetuate a symbol of power over the minority.

# Preparing for the Twelfth

Up Bishop Street
Around the corner
To the blackened door
Tap, tap

A doorman answers
Mumbled words
The door opens
Just enough to allow admittance
A quick glance both ways on Palace Street
Everyone, everything
Every shadow is under suspicion
Enter the dim light
Walls that have a sense of being
Because of their ugly colour
They have not seen paint in countless years
A mute television flashes images
Another irony
Stephen King's horror movie "It" flashes
An ugly head on the screen
Uneasy glances at the stranger
Who accompanies the locals?
Why are they here?
What will they think, say or do?
Are they friend or foe?
They sit uneasy for a few minutes
A man alone moves away
Is it the cigarettes the women smoke?

Or his suspicion?
The intruders talk among themselves
Relaxing with the alcohol
More drinks, more noise
The lack of colour becomes an
Intolerance to the artistic eye
But yet, perhaps that is its strength
A young man in his twenties becomes
Loud and obnoxious
His manner speaks of someone who is
"A few bricks short of a load"
He drinks cheap whiskey, straight up
Becomes louder and more aggressive
Beating a tattoo on the counter
Suddenly the sound of a tin whistle
Accompanies him
The tension in the room relaxes
As whistle and drum meld together
In an awkward sound of rhythm
The men begin to march and jest
Broomsticks and gloves
Par rum, par rum
Fife and drum
The drummer takes the lead
In his silly game of march and drum
The ladies with the cigarettes giggle at first
Then as the marchers

Becomes more rancorous
They laugh uncontrollably
At the fools of drink and war
Par rum, par rum
Around the bar
For a few minutes
The room is filled with laughter
Whistles and shouts
The barman afraid the party
Is getting out of hand
Calls "Time"
"Gentlemen, time"
The ladies with the cigarettes
Wipe away tears
Of laughter from their eyes
Gather up their purses and belongings
The television credits roll
For Stephen King's movie
It too is over
The walls close in
And the intruders politely
Call good night to
Their new companions
Men who say: "It was just for fun"
Stepping out into the city night
Causes them to pull coats near
At the corner they wait

Soldiers and police
Begin a quick assault
Past the merry makers
British soldiers with guns extended
Whisper into their jackets
Hurry down Bishop Street
Past the Diamond
They must intimidate
Some other revelers
Who are leaving the Derry Bars bars
All preparing for the Twelfth

Down Bishop Street
Around the corner
A door is opening
Tap, tap

*Londonderry/Derry*
*August 11, 1994*

## Shared Beginnings

When I first began my spiritual quest I prayed for guidance, someone to assist me along my spiritual path. As the old adage promised; "when the student is ready the teacher will come." My teacher was a woman on a similar journey of self-discovery. Though we were from two different cultures we became mentors to each other. We shared the same longing for the words of the Creator, calling her various names: God, Mother Earth, Goddess; sometimes we named ourselves as creator goddesses.

We were an unlikely match, I made homemade bread and wrote poetry; she created art and braided sweet grass. When I visited her home, her paintings caught my breath causing me to weep tears of joy. They showed me a vibrant world I had never before envisioned. It was a strange world filled with men and women who were spiritually connected to the earth.

I also brought gifts to our friendship with stories of a mysterious land and people whose true identity were unknown to her. Our families mingled. We shared salmon on New Year's Eve bringing special delicacies to the banquet table wrapped in the warmth of friendship. We celebrated the joys of creating with art and writing poetry.

From our journey we learned that both cultures, Maliseet and Irish, held similar creation stories. Our myths and legends had common threads woven through them. Our clans carried soil when they traveled sharing the belief that the soil holds the spirit of the land. She cared for me and led me in the rituals of the sweat lodge so that I would no longer fear confinement. With her by my side I was finally able to return to the womb of Mother Earth.

We traveled to Ireland together where I shared my culture and my people with her. At Newgrange we entered the ancient monument. In that sacred space we discovered that she had been to a similar lodge in America, which convinced us of our shared beginnings. We brought sweet grass to the border hills of Ireland and prayed for Peace.

Guiding the smoke upwards, we asked the eagle to return to the ancient land. Together we left our footprints in the earth, to speak to the Mother, so that she would know her children were present. Later my teacher-friend moved to a different place for a while and I missed her. Because of distance and time we did not visit or write often. Yet we were secure in the knowledge that our friendship would always remain strong because of the journey we had made together.

## Alive at Newgrange

In Ireland the world of ordinary reality exists side by side with the world of spirit. Both recognize and honour the presence of the other. The island itself is steeped in the mystery of ancient tribes that once inhabited the land. Christianity has learned to accept the worlds of the little people and the land of Tír na nÓg.

To honour the heritage of both Christian and Pagan cultures a stop at Saint Patrick's Cathedral must be followed by a visit to the Hill of Tara. Each god and goddess has its own place with sacred sites and offerings.

History tells us that long before the Celts came to Ireland many other tribes had inhabited the island. In a time long ago, the land of Erin was overtaken by a tribe from Greece, the tribe of the goddess Danu - the Tuatha Dé Danaan, 'the people of light'.

The tribe was a confederacy, in which kingship was determined by matrilineal succession. The invaders were depicted as accomplished soothsayers and necromancers, blessed with great powers that enabled them to quell storms, cure diseases, work with metals and foretell the future. Tribal leaders and bards forged magical weapons and, were reported on occasion, to raise the dead.

The tribe was also renowned for its supernatural powers, held by virtue of the *Lia Fáil* or Stone of Destiny. The tribe of the goddess Danu remained in Ireland for many years until displaced by the Milesians and Gaelic tribes, later to be known as the Celts.

The Tuatha Dé Danaan fought the Milesians and upon losing the battle of Moytura were said to have disappeared. Folklore tells us the conquered did not leave Ireland but sought to remain in their beloved land by retreating into the hills and mounds until such times as they were called to return to their rightful place. Their presence in Ireland is acknowledged still as "the little people" or "the children of light."

## Journey Home

### Stage I

Returning to this ancient land
I begin my journey
It is a long journey
One that will take a lifetime to complete
I come to this place in search of my soul
My mirror reflection
I seek the Goddess Danu
I seek the light
My heart pounds with anticipation
The same questions reverberate in my head
Over and over again
Who am I?
Where did I come from?
Who are my people?
Am I an alien being?
From the tribe of the Tuatha Dé Danaan
Did I once inhabit this place?

Am I but a spirit
In human form
Experiencing this material world for insight?
My senses are awake
When I am in this magical place
Every fibre of my body
Sings with joy
Feel the earth beneath my feet
Taste the wind
Hear the words of birds

I fly with them, up, up
Over, over the mountains
To the North, to the South
To the Grainian of Aileach
I am the earth
I am the sky
I am immortal
There are no answers
Only more questions

**Stage II**

Quiet, quiet, still, still
Words cannot bring answers
Words bring confusion
Silence, silence
Lay down, lay down
Sleep, sleep
The Mother enfolds me
Dream, dream
Quiet, dream, sleep
Fly, fly
Over land, over sea
Up, up
Rising into
Ether air
To awake, to awake
To begin again
To renew the journey

**Stage III**

Throughout this ancient land
There remain
Elements of a past
Familiar places
Familiar tastes
Sounds of tinkling bells
In the inner heart
My human body responds
To the essence
Here I am truly alive
Go, go
Back to the ancient mounds
Newgrange, Tara
Get off the bus
Leave the bus behind
Lay in the arms of Mother Earth
For here, here is where
Her heart remains
She is caught between the worlds
Like I
The struggle of spirit
And human form
Wanting to be free
But held back by those
Who do not believe
In her existence

## Stage IV

Awake, awake
Kind Mother
I kneel at your fountains
And streams
I need no altar
Nor church spire
For I have the
Blue sky overhead
For my mantle

## Stage V

Enter the cave of
Wonderment
Enter the stone passage
Feel every fibre of the human body
Resonate to the energy
Held between the stones
The passage is narrow
And cold
Breathe, breathe the
Life breath
Release, release the air
In lungs exploding
Aha, aha, we enter
The cave of life
We enter the birthing room

We are alive and the
Cycle begins again
Birth, death, life
There are no answers
Only more questions

**Stage VI**

Inside the birthing room
I gather up my human clothes
To begin the journey
Back to reality
For I understand
That I am from
The ancient tribe of the
Goddess Danu
The Children of Love
Here, to bring light
To those who question
And do not believe
Sleep, sleep
Quiet, quiet
The story ends
The circle
Begins, again

*Newgrange*
*County Meath*

# Circles of Time and Place

# Douglas Avenue 1944

Clang, clang
Streetcar memories
Steeple houses
Oval windows
Opaque stained glass
Carriages and ladies
A child with green eyes
Watches her world fly by

The streetcar
Rumbles, bumbles
Past the museum
Follow the stairs
To the school on the hill
Pace quickening
Trees line the avenue
Flowers and memories
The streetcar reaches
The bridge

Clang, clang
Childhood visions
Of the falls below
She clutches her Mother's hand
At four she can never bear
To cross the bridge
They round the corner
On Douglas Avenue

Aunt Helen's house
Tiled walls
Cut glass windows
Grandmother's china
Mind your manners child
Sit up straight
Do not hunch your shoulders
Come to tea

Kiss Aunt Greta, dear
Remember
Always be a lady
Clang, clang
The streetcar
Takes her home

*Saint John*
*New Brunswick*

## Heathrow Airport

Istanbul, Mumbai
New York, San Francisco
Stockholm, Newark, Miami
Bahrain, Riyadh Doha and Frankfurt
The public address system continues
To call the names
Politely repeating the chant
Only the select few may travel
All others are obliged
To wait in the lounge
Until their flight is called

Travelers gather at Heathrow
From every space on earth
Collecting their material self
In suitcases and plastic bags
Surrounded by the symbols
Of earth's pleasures
Chanel, Bally, Gucci shoes and Boots
The pharmaceutical conspirators
Who aid in this distortion of life

The loudspeaker repeats itself
Calling new names
Of other distant cities
The message remains
Please wait in the lounge
For your flight to be called
Until visualization is apparent
Wait for the world to unfold
Detailing the next reality
And the flight for Toronto

*London*

# Flying

In the distance
I can see the Austrian Alps
Snow covered
Early morning light
I remember the journey
Musicians in Vienna
Artists in Paris
Philosophers in Berlin
Each city
A place for dreamers

## Paris Night

I feel compelled to tell you
I carry you with me
Often words or phrases appear
And I remember Paris
And the night
The lights and the river
Dark and foreboding
Twice around the Esplanade
To see the men dressed as women
Fast past the trees in the park
To the book store where Hemingway
hung out
(You knew I would like that place)
There were no photos taken
Because it was night
Yet I keep photos in my mind
Calling them up on occasion
Remembering Paris, the night and you
I smile at the image

# Vienna

In Vienna
The sky is blue
But that is not true
Perhaps, now blue sky
Solar powered cars
Dogs that are on a leash
Groomed, well mannered and cultured
Cars flow to a rhythm
No horns blaring
A girl darts out in front of traffic
Tempting fate
Her friend is more cautious
Goes to the pedestrian walk
A cyclist sounds his bell
A pleasant br..rring, br..rring
A childhood sound
Philosophers come to this place
Of order and culture
To seek truth
Appealing to the enlightened
Poets pause to question
What is enlightenment?
Blue trucks, white vans
This is a civilized place
One of culture and order

Tour buses follow
Around a traffic ring
In slow motion
Picking up the beat of a city
Where the sky is blue
Or is that only today's reality
In this moment of time

## Pompeii

In the House of the Golden Bracelet
Selene reigns supreme
Goddess of the night
She watches over
The women of the villa
As they gather
For their morning bath
Ladies of wealth
Servants carry warm oils
And scents of lavender
They prepare for the day
A spa – a place of luxury
Suddenly the clouds change
The earth shakes —

## The Blue Lagoon

In spite of its romantic title, The Blue Lagoon is one of the world's most deplorable environmental disaster areas. Without research it can only be described in layman's terms as a former chemical plant where toxic, radioactive wastes were dumped into lagoons when the Soviet Union abandoned Estonia at the end of the Cold War.

In the former Soviet days, James Bond himself would have a problem getting into the plant area. Now, tourists out to visit the beach can drive nonchalantly around the town and through the gates into the train yard of the former plant.

Gates hang ajar, broken and useless. The yards are vacant except for a man pushing a baby carriage. As we pass, we notice there is no child inside but rather the carriage is filled with coal from the abandoned plant. Soviet brick and concrete buildings dot the desolate landscape. Long lengths of huge piping straddle buildings from one to the other while in other areas conveyer belts dot the sky between obsolete buildings. Massive buildings wander everywhere without rhyme or reason with wide doors ajar or missing, windows absent or broken.

The place is huge covering vast acres of land with winding roads and broken pavement that lead us around one building to another. We can only guess that the lagoon is off somewhere to the right near the sea. A white car behind merely ignores us and turns away, probably a local taking a short cut.

There are no guards or sentries only signs hanging askew, swinging in the wind. We approach a rise, which turns out to be a slagheap. Overhead steel tracks lead nowhere and hang in mid-air.

We pause to get out of the car. Carefully we climb the hill. In the distance we see the ponds. We are reminded that a veteran scientist with knowledge of nuclear waste would only approach this site with nothing less than a space suit covering his body.

Our guide allows us a few moments to see what is in front of us encouraging us not to stay long, he is anxious to retreat. I hesitate and rummage in my medicine bag for offerings. We have no tobacco as none of us smoke. Instead I bring forth clean soil from my garden at home. I remember; "earth carries spirit." I also have sage. I call the wind to take the message to Mother Earth. We have come because we believe and offer our miniscule prayer for her healing. The wind comes up and sweeps the sage from my hands. We are all very quiet sensing the intensity of the ritual and the acknowledgement of the gift.

We are silent as we leave unprepared for the enormity of the scene before us. The next hour and half we circle the area looking for higher ground to view the lagoons. The sea cliffs surround the area so the detour takes us some time.

We find a bunker where we view four lagoons separated by piles of earth and shale, the one closest to us is a thick deep green, a hideous green slime. The sea surrounds the lagoons and when the waves are even slightly high it is inevitable that the water washes over them and carries the toxins out into the sea. The others are indeed blue, a hideous substance hard to describe as the water laps against the lagoons leaching the dreaded chemicals out into the sea.

In complete contrast to the view on the left, the sun is setting against the Baltic Sea with vermillion, yellow and gold with wisps of clouds that paint a scene of beauty to distract us from what we witnessed from the bunker moments before.

With the setting sun we leave The Blue Lagoon in search of our Bed and Breakfast in a seaside town that, in its former glory, was the home of the aristocracy. During the Second World War, it became the scene of some of the most horrible of battles. Our eyes are directed to the trees that still hold fragments of shrapnel, all still painful and unforgiving, wounds that cannot heal. This is the road to Narva. That evening I wrote, “Here’s to the Blue Lagoon.”

I have carried parts of Estonia home with me, small tangible gifts from the land and its people: Two books, meteorite rocks, a butterfly, photos, and the inevitable Russian stacking dolls. I have also brought with me the spiritual gift of a deeper understanding of how a land and its people can survive untold oppression, fear, and sadness, and yet rise from the ashes to sing again. They are a strong and noble people.

About six months later I received word from Estonia that the Baltic States had come to an agreement to send in experts to somehow begin to clean up the Blue Lagoon. Our prayers were answered.

*October 1999*

# Here's to the Blue Lagoon

Candle light
Chilled wine
Soft Music
Cigarette smoke
Tinges the air
Distant music
Blue flag over City Hall
Climb the ramparts
Leave behind
The scene of the Blue Lagoon
It belongs to another place
A dream of another world
Not to be confused with this one
This is a place of music and song

*Narva, Estonia*
*October 1999*

## Skating to Narva

Learning the way of the Shaman
We walk the path of history
From Kuressaare to Paldiski
We feel and hear with our senses
But do not understand the
Madness that is around us
From Kuressaare to Paldiski
We travel paved highways
Past wooden farm houses
With no colour nor design
Faded and bleached from time
We look for birds
Even they do not arrive
A few ravens enter our space
Falling down from castle walls
Swans enter our view
Those who wait for autumn flight
From Kuressaare to Paldiski
We watch and wait
For the river to freeze
So we can skate to Narva
But there is no joy in Narva
Only Russians on either side of the border
Countrymen divided by a customs station
Who try to ignore the posters that declare
Do not enter
It is a strange place
Here where the fire burned
Leaving only scorched earth

Humans, they continue to wander in a daze
From Kuressaare to Paldiski
Spirit rises to the sky
No one wants to skate again to Narva

*Estonian/Russian border at Narva*
*October 1999*

# Tallinn

Inside the ancient wall
The wars continue
Schoolboys with shaven heads
Black boots, leather jackets
Replace the soldiers
Of former days
They lean against
The walls on an autumn day
Plotting yet a new war
A war of conspiracy
Against authority
Parents, police and their piers
Become the enemy
They swagger past tourists
Cursing their presence
Jealous of their freedom
Soon, soon they swear
They too will escape the walls
Of this ancient town
Learn all there is to
Know of life
They will go to the University of Tartu
To become the new Estonia

They will leave behind
The black boots
Shaven heads
To be replaced
By Hugo Boss suits and a Volvo
Then they will become
The controllers of power
Within the fiefdom
Of this kingdom
Power begets power
Fear begets fear
Nowhere do we see love
In the equation

*Tallinn, capital city of Estonia*

# Tent City Orange Revolution

In the Tent City
The young girl
Smiles broadly
As the camp commander
Acknowledges
"She has been
Here since day one."
A camera appears
We stand together
I a stranger
And the girl
We do not understand
Each other's language
I look into her eyes
A mother,
I hold her in my arms
Beneath the heavy coat
She trembles
And lets go of the fear
She has had since it all began
I take an amulet
From my neck
And put it around hers

A medal for a heroine
Whose name I do not know
Whose language I cannot speak
The moment etched in memory
For a lifetime

    The camera clicks

*Kiev, Ukraine*
*December – January, 2004*

# Chisinau, Moldova

Sitting on a street in Chisinau
Looking for poetry
City sounds, horns
Car alarms all harsh
Russian language
Pedestrians with eyes down
Serious, sad
Flowers reluctant to bloom
Impatient drivers
In a hurry to go nowhere
The car horn their only weapon
Against the world
In their haste
They keep banging
Into each other
Symbolic of the city itself
No clear destination
Only bumper car mentality
Round and round
Hit as many cars (or people)
As you can at one go
For the poet, it is not
For me to judge
Yet to be human

I imagine
The trees are the only
Beings on the street impervious
To the haste and waste
They watch the people come and go
Along the route to Odessa
Odessa is on every signpost
As if it were the only way to freedom
That is the city of Chisinau

*Spring 2004*

# Moldova Park

## Scene 1

Wedding in the park
White sashes
Carnations for the hero of the state
Stephan de Mare
Priest in white

## Scene 2

Young man and woman
On green bench
Clutch each other
Hand on thigh
Lips, tongues
Spring is in the air

## Scene 3

Church, priest
Bride in white net
Mary Poppins image
Ready to fly
Red carnations
Tribute to a nation
In this world
Of communism

## Scene 4

Man pushing a pram
Woman walks separate, detached
Dressed in leather pants
High stiletto heels
What will become of the child?
The infant of a country
Without order
Without a mother

## Knossos, Crete

The bull dancers
Return each morning
As tour guides
They wonder what draws them
Back to this place of antiquity
Dressed in mini-skirts and stiletto heels
They traverse the Palace of Knossos
Day after day
Repeating the vigil
Repeating the dance

# Paros - Monday Morning

The cerulean blue sea
Washes the shores of Paros
On Monday mornings
While tourists
Tired from an evening of wine
At Christos
Wash their belongings
Hang them to dry on balconies
Unaware that soon
The western winds from Italy
Will blow ships, laundry and tourists
Off to Mykonos
For another night of dancing
Along the Aegean Sea

*Greece*

# Mykonos

Spelling defies the brain
A new story emerges
A love story
Pattie purchased a love boat
In Mykonos
But would not
Unwrap it
Until she returned home
Love waits patiently

*Greece*

# Delos

Delos Tours
Dolphins
Cinema
German bikers
Market
Feathered clouds
Deep, dark, blue sea
Place of the Gods
Apollo
Artemis

*Greece*

## Santorini

There must be many poems
About Santorini
A poem for each visitor
Who comes to this strange land
An island of rock and volcanic ash
Where even grapevines cling
Close to the earth
To defy the constant winds
That blow over this island
At the far end of the lava base
The city of Akrotiri lies buried
Holding on to its secret
It would appear to some
That the ancient Atlanteans
Have returned
To live in Oia
Or in the city of Thera
In a series of white doomed caves
That defies gravity
And cling to a rock face
Presenting an idyllic scene
For tourist brochures
The truth hidden beneath the layers
Upon layers of antiquity
Each holding the mystery of the past

*Greece*

# Saturday is the Day for Leaving

A time for fast ferries
A return to 'civilization'
No more island dreams
Buried cities
Island sanctuaries
Grecian Gods
Or meetings with Panto,
The mayor of Piccolo
By fast ferry we leave for Athens
For yet another adventure
Fine hotels with hot water
Taxi service
Gods now confined to museums
Instead of an island
City sounds and homeward bound
We leave behind the dream of Santorini

*Greece*

# The Beach

The ocean washes
Men's sins upon the shore
Remnants of the night
Glass bottles
Plastic cups
Gnarled fishing nets
Flotsam and jetsam
Ebb and flow

Eyes are drawn away
By the daily debris
On this island paradise
Trojan signs, horse hoof prints
Mingle with broken shells

Ebb and flow
Ebb and tide
Break away
From the debris
Hear only sound
Heart beat
Cast your eyes south
For the noon day sun
Waves wash against a red shore
Feet imprint the sand
A tiny bird like trail

The waves wash behind
Wiping out my existence
Overhead a 747 clears
Liahue airport
A reminder of my leaving
The sun kisses my face
A reminder of staying
The heart is confused
The irony of sand and debris
Are there no lessons to be learned?

Who cast a Corona bottle
On this sacred shore?
Those who come
Do they not respect the earth?
Ebb and tide
Ebb and flow
The ocean waves cast
Men's sins upon the shore

*Kauai*
*Hawaii*

# Boats Along the River Dart

Boats struggle to free themselves
Along the River Dart
Each maneuver for time/space
They move in unison
In the October wind
Tourists and students
Have left the park
To seek new adventures
Leaving the boats empty and alone
They rock back and forth
Waiting for a sunny Sunday
When the revellers will return
To hoist their sails
Escape to the outer sea
And freedom

*Totnes*
*England*

## Green-Apple Dress

Crystal children
Bright colors
Pinks, purples
Green-apple dress
Multilingual children
From all over the globe
Familiar sounds
But strange words
Crying child in a dragon cape
On Bank Street
The smell of honeysuckle
A stick in the water
Floats down the canal
Soccer game
A girl with long braids
Tends goal
Unafraid of being a tomboy
Names called: Ella, Grace
Lily, Arden, Hudson, Rory
Liam and Ivy
Markusha tells me, it is time
To read to his class
Children of the world
Unite in a kindergarten class

*Ottawa*
*May 2010*

## Costume Ball

For a brief moment
The guests were able
To waltz
Out of time
Transcend the material world
Escape the past
Led by an aviator
With a foreign accent
He entered the room
A romantic figure
With his well worn boots
Scuffed from ages of travel
Who as a child dreamed
That he would fly
Transformed by a silk scarf
And Billy Bishop's flight goggles
He transported the guests
Into his dream

Women of another century
With busts uplifted
Sauntered through
Exposing themselves
To the evening guests
They were figures from history books
Who moved through the assembly
While waiters with goblets of wine
Mingled with the intoxicant
To keep the illusion alive

Nellie McClung competed for center stage
With a young Queen Victoria
A group of Trekies
With teleporters
Strapped to their arms

Adjusted to the time warp
The observers of the evening
Transfixed by the scene
Asked if it was
An alcoholic induced space
That has caused them to believe
They had left reality behind.

To add to the delusion
Scarlet-coated Mounties
Escorted John A. MacDonald
Through the assembly
The audience awaited the next scene
Like credits on a movie screen
They sauntered into a hall
Of smoke and mirrors
Wandering into a space
Transformed by glow balls
Encountering dancers gyrating
To an unusual beat
Perhaps a rhythm of the future
As the patrons of the costume ball
Entered the fifth dimension

*Museum of Civilization*
*Ottawa, 2006*

## Finding Our Voice

During the CAIS conference
At the University of Toronto
A stranger from Ireland asked of me:
"Who are the great poets of Canada?"
A Canadian goose walking alongside of us
Interrupted our conversation
I hesitated,
My subconscious alert to the symbol walking beside me
I pondered the question, wanting to say
"I shall be that great poet!"
But knowing that would never happen
I replied:
"We are only now finding our voice!"
I am as surprised as the stranger
At my response
I do not retract my words
Instead my mind searches for poems
That would be recognized
By listeners of Morningside

We Canadians of intellect,
Are defined by the CBC
Radio, not television
It holds the key to our identity
We are a nation shaped by names like Gzowski,
Called to order over morning coffee
To declare our loyalty on such subjects as politics,
The weather, economics and the Dead Dog Café

We test our sense of place in the world
By Lewis, Axworthy and DeChastelain
Who are we are, where do we go
Our identity punctuated by hockey scores
And the Great Games
The time we beat the Russians
Finally, the Gold at the Olympics
Our identity soars, we are on top of the heap
Our sense of place in the world identified by
Hockey pucks and Moosehead beer
We are content with this place
In the greater scheme of things
We have no notion to be world leaders
But rather world savers
Conscious of our maternal notion of
Taking care of the earth
Our femininity secure, we need only hockey players
To defend our honour
For we fear neither oppression nor war
Celebrating instead great open spaces
Rivers that flow
And a sure sense of our own identity
We are the poets of the land

## Time Moves Quickly

Time

Moves

Quickly

While I cling to earthly things

Time, which has no meaning
Confines my days and nights
Time marked by
Days, months and years
Clicks like rosary beads
Each bead a segment
Of my string of realities

Like the mysteries of the beads
Sometimes sorrow, often mystery
Occasionally joy
All fingered
And held in unison
A pattern of
Beginnings and endings

Time measured in
    Decades
    Birth, life, death

This year beginning
    In joy
It will continue in the
    Joyful mysteries
Encased in time

*January 2014*

# In Dreams Begin the Courage of the Spirit

## Strange Land

We were, in ancient times,
But clumps of earth
That had gotten up
And began to sing
In modern days
We have forgotten earth
And now believe
We are the song
Yet each journey takes us back
To the land of our beginnings
Where we ache for a familiar sound
We ask for words, a vibration
Anything that will heal
The ache in our soul
But the earth remains silent
Has she too forgotten the song?

*Inishowen Tour*
*New Brunswick*
*1992*

## Night Sky

There are those who say
We are made from stardust
I want to believe them
For I have no fear of death
Knowing that I would be cast
Upon the blanket sky
Ever present
Watching over
My love

# Venus

Each night as she travels
Across the sky from east to west
Venus pulls at the hearts
Of those who seek her attention
Those who know her
Try to seduce her with love potions
Lavender and anise
Mixed with erotic spices from the orient
Trying to control an energy that is uncontrollable
She continues on her path without concern
Following an eight year cycle
A pattern of the labyrinth below
Meanwhile the goddess of love selects
Her subjects without their knowledge
There is no human capable
Of understanding Venus
Nor her apprentice Eros
As they wander the night sky
Seeking victims for their play

# Full Moon in September

The ladies of Johnville
are putting out their crystals
Drawing down the energy
of the full moon in September
We have come far in our evolution
From rosary beads to crystals
Each symbol seeking the energy
Of God, Goddess, Spirits
Man, woman, searching for answers
And control in a universe
We can never understand

*Johnville*
*Carleton County*
*New Brunswick*

## Feathers and Shells

I give you a swan's feather
For I am unable to fly away with you
I give you a song
For I cannot speak to you
I give you a seashell
For I am unable to give you material gifts
I weave you a dream
For I am unable to give you reality
If feathers and shells will hold you
Then I will come to you in dreams
And sing you a song
With words and melodies
That will never end

# Meditation

The Tibetan bells
Signal
A call to order
A lining up of the chakras
A body in attunement
The sun peeks in my room
Looking to see
Where the sound originates
I sit with housecoat
And floppy slippers
Exploring the world
The scene
Interrupted by cat
Jumping on to the table
Singeing his fur
In the flame of a candle
Sacrificing himself
To alert me
To the dangers of the world

*The Farm*
*Johnville, New Brunswick*

## After September 11, 2001

Everything has changed
No matter where you live
No matter how powerful
Or how weak
Planet Earth has ruptured
From deep beneath its bowels
Spewing out a force
That cannot be altered
Nor contained
From the fire
The phoenix will rise again
Given time and circumstance
The shape to be determined
By earth soul and consciousness
A new pattern will emerge
Blue flags will fly
As well as red and green
United under a noonday sun
Giving brilliance to a
New world order of
Peace, love and hope
For those who will
Hold the image of brilliant light
In their mind's eye

*Schumacher College*
*Dartington, England*

# Contemplating the War in Iraq

*Morning, winter continues to breath heavily upon us. Cold biting wind with no respite, only nights of fear and the unknown outside our sleeping dens. The weather reflects the uncertainty of the war in Iraq as we huddle for comfort beneath quilts of eider down...*

With the sun
Hope rises
News comes
Of peace marches
But cold winds
Dash protesters to the ground
Words from Paris
Suggest a compromise
But rising oil prices
Indicate war

The wind blows
North to east
Bringing changes to
The drifts of snow
Outside my window
A morning radio broadcast
Changes my mood of optimism
Dashing it to a somber
Pessimistic
Attitude of despair

Seeking answers
I retreat to meditation
Playing Bach and
Hildegard Von Bingen
Bingen, said to be the nearest sound
On earth
To the voice of angels
The world needs a
Host of angels
If we are to survive
This winter of discontent

*2003*

## Morning Light

I dream of change
Yet none comes
I dream of knights and
Wait for sunrise
I dream of adventure
And rainbows appear
I dream of love
And Pan appears
I wait for magic
And see the stars
Against a perfect sky
I count the flowers
In my garden
They freeze at night
I wait for warm days
The flowers return
I go to the river
And watch for dolphins
Water fairies appear
They call the dolphins near
The dolphins leap in joy
I send them light
From my heart centre

## Water Fairies

Water fairies
Beyond our reach
Glistening
Far off
In the distant river
Our hearts reach out
To touch them
Feel their embrace
Aching for a summer past
Sun warm against our face
The river ice
Closing in upon us
Blocking our path
Water fairies
Please return to us
Our hearts
Are frozen in time

*Saint John River*
*Woodstock, New Brunswick*

## Nature Spirits

I have not seen them
But they are here
I can feel them in my bones
Smell them in the night
Amidst their evening flower flight
Devas of another world
Who flit from bush to bloom
Among the sacred groves
Pulling buds into flower
Leaves into light
Each a job to do
Farmers of the night

*The Farm*
*Johnville, New Brunswick*

## Cosmic Dance

Hidden deep
Within the Dartmoor woods
Are Fairies
Beneath a waterfall
They circle round
In delight
Circulating light
They create a vortex
Spiraling upwards
To Sky then down
To Earth
They honour our presence
As we pass
We leave chocolate
Beneath the trees
To acknowledge their presence
As we seek our own rhythm
To join them
In the cosmic dance

*Dartmoor, UK*
*Fall, 2001*

## Message

Fairies all hear my call
The time has come
For one and all to gather near
Our words are needed
Our voices to be heard
Above the cities roar
With magick to reveal
To soothe and heal
The aching heart of earth

## Loneliness

The birds and I sit alone
Out here in the wilderness
The setting sun
Creates an aura
On the mantle
Of the earth

The sky shows evidence of the day
With chemtrails over clouds
Tearing at the seams of whiteness
Strange birds retreat to an
Unknown hideaway
They systematically fly each evening
Following earth clock time

Smaller birds follow in their wake
To hide among the branches of a large tree
The birds, the trees are foreign to me
For I am a stranger in this place
I bend down beneath the willow tree
To caress the earth
And leave my tears behind

*Swan Lake*
*Florida*
*2012*

# On Hearing of Brian Goodwin's Passing

The drum beats
The heart beats
Encased in glass
The drum is silent
The heart beats
The drum will beat again
To the rhythm
Of a new drummer

*Schumacher College, 2001*

## Life Path

It matters not
What dreams we seek
Or secrets we are bound to keep
The path we take
Will circle round
Above our heads
And below the ground
To come back true
And meet us in a spiral
At the very point
Where the path began

## Altar

Stone upon stone
Feather upon sand
Light upon metal
I build my altar

Oak leaves and sage
Crystal and water
Earth and prayer flag
Candle and spirit

Earth spirits
Enter the room
I feel their presence
With a heaviness on my shoulders

I carry the burden
As it holds the security
Of another dimension
Of time and place

A place where
I long to enter
A place of contentment
The door remains closed

Until I am ready
To take my assigned place
On the wheel of my
Life's journey

## Red Crane Against the Moon

Grandmother Moon
Tell us your secrets
So we will be able to save the world
We gather under a vibrant sky
Waiting for the message of the ancestors

Heart Beat, Drum Beat

We share the earth
Bare feet feel the touch
Earth Mother knows us
She tells us the stories of our ancestors

The stories are the same for each of us
All contained in the Crane Bag
We share the same wind
Salmon from the clear waters give us wisdom
We carry spirit in the earth as we wander
Seeking a better life for our children

Heart Beat, Drum Beat

Together we unite under the sky
All reaching for the same knowledge
All believing in the same Gods
Creation Mother, Earth Mother, Sister Sky
We ask for your blessings
We are descendants of the Children of Light
Children of the new dawn rising

# Seasons of Words on the Edge of Silence

# Words of Advice from My Father

There is no rhythm or rhyme to my words
Only staggering thoughts misspelled & abbreviated
The melody is not clear, the meaning obscure
Even to a poet looking for a voice
My father comes to me and whispers in my ear just as he
Did when I was twelve when he taught me how to dance

"Listen, feel the beat in your feet
Feel the beat in your heart
Feel the vibration in your body
Listen feel pause
Wait it will come
The waltz will return
If you are patient"

## Ellen's First Bowl

The bowl is empty
The bowl is full

The bowl holds water
The bowl holds air
The bowl is made from earth
Fired in a blazing kiln

The bowl is a symbol
Of all of the elements
Fire, earth, water and air
The bowl is sacred

Made with love
The bowl is soft
To the touch
Of the potter's hand

The bowl is cooled
From the owner's embrace
The bowl changes the room
When it is put upon the table

Filled with fruit
It brings an air of abundance
Grapes drape its side
Giving an air of Grecian Dionysus

The bowl is filled
With sunflowers and gourds
Orange and watery yellow
Fall is coming

The bowl is filled with acorns
Pinecones and nuts
Silver tinsel
Christmas beckons

The bowl is filled with packages
Asters, sweet mallow
And nasturtium seeds
Awakening spring

The bowl holds the center
Of the universe
The bowl holds my world
Encased in ceremony

The bowl is empty
The bowl is full

# Ocean Images

Purple asters
Little crab—metamorphous
Footprints in the sand
Bare feet, freedom
Sharp grass
Tangled rope
Water fairies
Dancing in the afternoon sun
White butterfly
In a hurry
Filling in the moments
Left of summer

*Bay of Fundy Shore*
*New Brunswick*

## Modern World

Today is an important day
For our family
One child is being married
Another is getting a divorce
Such is the way of the modern world

We have no control
Parents over children
Husbands over wives
Governments over its citizens

Under the flag of freedom
We cry out for justice
Die for the right to vote
For the man (sic) of our choice
Then mock him after he is elected

Allow me to smoke in public
Children suffer from asthma
Give me the freedom to write what I want
Children mimic the words
Shooting classmates in their seats

We are spiraling into the next dimension
Seeking individual rights
The ability to make choices
The freedom of self
Such is the way of the modern world

## Irish Conference

The speaker
Has allowed the power point
Machine to remain on
Pasting letters on his forehead
Letters that move about
On his face
Backward o's and n's
Together they spell
Irish Nationalism

Here at this select conference
Of distant Irish patriots
In Newfoundland
A "real" Irishman explains
The history of his race
With letters etched
On his forehead
The strength of his words
Lost in the irony of the scene

*Canadian Association*
*of Irish Studies Conference*
*St. John's, Newfoundland*
*2007*

## Winter Questions

Who will feed the birds
When I am gone
Who will see to their daily habits
Of oatcakes and sunflower seeds
Who will attend to the chickadees
Who come to my hand for crumbs
The cat too needs my attention
Who will give him milk when
I am gone
We go to the door to spread seeds and corn
For the adventurous blue jays and grosbeaks
Who come to the feeder
Cat retreats quickly
As the winter wind circles
Around us
Like me he is getting old
Content to remain
Inside the glass
Allow the birds their freedom
He and I both dream of past days
Intent on the hunt
We no longer care if the prey
Gets away
We remember our victories
As we retreat to the fire
To wait for spring

*The Farm*
*Johnville, New Brunswick*

## Winter

Winter is a waiting period
Clean and white
Crisp and crunchy
A time for reflection
And no direction
Standing in a place
Of stillness
Opening to thoughts
A time to wait for words
For glimmers of light
A time for hibernation
To form seeds and grow roots
To feel the bitter cold
And prepare for change

*The Farm*
*Johnville, New Brunswick*

## Winter Contentment

This is the winter of contentment
A time to remain inside
And view the world
From behind the glass
Cars go by as nurses go to work
Men drive logging trucks to the mill
My job is to remain here
Still and quiet and meditate
On the grander scheme of things
To read philosophy
Feed the birds
Feed the cat
And prepare supper
For the workers
I must define my space
And my place
In individual ways
I seek words
And perfect sentences
To validate my existence
And pay for my bread

*The Farm*
*Johnville, New Brunswick*

# Ice Queen

There is no way
I can write of anything
Besides winter
It surrounds my existence
I beg for other images
Blue skies, sandy beaches, swaying palms
But none appear
My world is encased in ice
The color white
Snow and wind
Shapes me
I learn to move
With its energy
I am not afraid
To be called
Ice Queen
She is who I am
A Canadian woman
Spirit of Windigo

## New Beginnings

I continue to give myself
New beginnings
Fresh starts
Renewed energy
Clean pages
New ideas
Fresh attitudes
Books on self-help

Encouragement for the ultimate dream
A dream that never changes
But I don't try
Fear of failure
Fear of what
Turn around
face yourself

I know it is coming
I can feel it in my bones
Begin the job
Raise the vibration
Leave the critics
And doubters behind
Be brave
Be bold
You are perfection

## Patricia's Dahlias

Patricia has thrown sheets
Over her dahlias
Protection against an early frost
I return to the farm
And contemplate the action
I would never bother with sheets
But instead, allow nature
To take its course
Being grateful for the relief
From the work of summer
Fall is a time for rest
I will be glad
When the geraniums
Are put to rest in the basement
But then I remember—
Patricia goes for chemotherapy
In the morning
If I were in Patricia's shoes
Perhaps I too
Would cover my dahlias
With white sheets

## A Writer's Room

This is my room
Strangers are forbidden
Children keep out
This is my private space
Where memories are buried
Deep beneath piles of papers
Stories are covered with bric-a-brac
Whirly gigs and broken pencils
Epic tales of love and life
Are stuffed into cardboard boxes
Tales of journeys not yet taken
Stories of castles yet to be built
Flow over the edges of wicker baskets
Waiting to be released to the universe

This is my room
My place to dream
Where photos of mountains
Yet to climb hang on the walls
Filing cabinets hold empty folders
Clean white paper
Historical notes on items from A to Z
They wait there in case of necessity
Intentions are placed firm
With color-coded push pins
On a bulletin board

They list my future
Poems published
Query letters sent
Manuscripts edited
Postage paid
My world of success
Encased in this space
The door remains ajar

## Friendship

Who else could I share my words
Except you
Who else would listen to the
Stillness of my heart
A breath, a pause
An instant so perfect
That I hold my breath
Words flutter from
Ether air
And then
By magic
Appear on paper
Clear and white
Perfect thoughts
A poem
That will unite us
Perfect friends

# Delirium

Where have all my poems gone?
I have lost my true voice
My sense of being
Words used to define me
Secret moments
Special thoughts
Tucked inside my physical self
Now I have become a void
Waiting for the sun to shine
Waiting for something
That will shake me out of this delirium

Delirium, a word I can hardly spell
Without the aid of spell check
But alas everything has changed
My words are the words of a machine
What does it matter?
Rambling helps when you are at the bottom
Of a pile of guilt, hopeless
Everything comes pouring out
Just when you least expect it

Where have my poems all gone?
The joy of life
The joie de vivre
Are they buried in the machine
That can no longer hear a heart beat?
This whole exercise is useless
Except for the fact
That I have learned
How to spell the word
Delirium

# Political Reflections in Spring

As the sun rises
And yellow finches
Queue up in the lilac bush
I am startled by the sharp
Call of the returning geese overhead

Spring returns with illusive sun
Days of rain and discomfort
Cold showers, flurries
As ferns reach out for warmth
Mornings are disrupted by the news
From our nation's capital
There is hatred and anger in the words
Hurled from neighbor to neighbor
They, like the honking of the geese,
Want to alarm us
Want to be heard
Even the birds are part of the conspiracy
To make the "house fall"

Nursery rhymes come to mind
"I'll huff and I'll puff
Until I blow your house in!"
Name calling, lies and more lies
Yet no one stands to defend peace
No one stands with the decorum of a leader
And circles the room with eyes and voice
And takes control
If there is to be peace in the nation
There must first be peace in the house
If there is to be peace in the house
There must be peace in the heart
Sit down, be still and listen
To the silence of peace

*The Farm*
*Johnville, New Brunswick*

# Selling Land

How is it we can sell land?
It is not a tangible object
Can I take this land to another place?
May I put it on a mantel and admire its beauty?
Land is attached to its surroundings
The trees the rivers
How can I own this piece of earth and rock?
How can I say it is mine?

I can only move around on the top of it
And use it wisely
Plant seed beneath the soil
And ask Mother Earth's permission
To allow its growth
If I were I to ask her
"Can I sell this land
To another?"
What would she say!

"It is not yours to give,
Only yours for a short time
So use it wisely
Love it as you would
Your own body
By honoring the land
You honour me."

## A Reluctant Spring

Winter and spring
Embrace outside my window
In the starlit night
I witness snow then rain
In the morning
I run to the window
To see who has won the battle
Snow covers the trees
Spring has retreated yet again to wait
For another night
As winter devours April

*The Farm*
*Johnville, New Brunswick*

## To Eamon Baker

Your heart is hanging in my window
The sunlight catches it and reflects colors
Colors of chakras, rainbows and love
A gentle breeze sneaks past me
Turning your heart around in sunlight
Light forms tease my eyes away from duty
As I turn to catch a glimpse of you
Ever present in my mind

# Sand Crane

Transfixed by the sound
The sand crane
Stood motionless
In the afternoon sun
Listening to my meditation tape
Tibetans bells
Archturian chant
Fixed on the sound
His head attentive
He turns to the sky
To my door
Seeking the source
Of this New Age sound
The vibration going out
Over the swimming pool
Of my winter home
Strange sound, strange place
The crane and I
Adjusting to the awakening
Of the new world vibration

*Swan Lake*
*Florida*

## Red Book

Is this little book
Big enough,
To hold a poem

Are the lines
Steady and straight
Enough
To carry words

It takes strength
And courage
To release energy
Into ether air

Exposing oneself
To the world at large
Thoughts transferred
To form, on paper

Ancient scribbling
Black ink
No computer
Or hieroglyphics

This little book
Was purchased
In the Back to School section
Of a Wexford stationary shop

I was on a walk about
A stranger in a foreign land
Looking for clues
To my destiny

I sought solace
By writing poetry
In a little book
With a shiny red cover

*Wexford, Ireland*
*2004*

# Vintage Wine

Poems written in journals
Age with time
Like vintage wine
They settle and wait
Secreted away in scribblers
To be discovered
Beneath the covers
Light glimmers
On their lines
Each line
A sip, a taste
To be savored
A memory of a day
On the vine
In the summer sun

# The Bath Meeting House

As the evening began
There was only the silence
Of a soft summer night
Cricket sounds, murmurs from the river

The poet stood on stage
The gathering came to hear her words
They did not know her
Even though she had lived among them
For almost sixty years

Oh, they knew the mother, friend, and neighbor
But few knew of her exotic travels
To places like Estonia, Totnes and Transnistria
Or of the time
She was followed by the KGB
Woman of the world
She traveled in disguise

Once she was in an accident in an embassy car
The paramedic referred to her in Russian as
"Someone's mother!"
She smiled as she translated his words
In her mind
Deep in her heart she knew
She was there as a undercover agent
For the Earth Mother
Leaving light crystals
In her wake

She had stories to tell
Places to go and perhaps
Just perhaps
Borders to heal
But that was then
And in the here and now
A chair moved
Metal striking metal

The audience came to attention
What poem will she read?
World traveler who hides
Away on a farm in the country
Witness to other dimensions
She stands at centre stage
Confident and in control
The room on the edge of silence
Waiting for her to expose herself

Through the open doors
The river urges her on

*Carleton County*
*New Brunswick*

# Notes

*Hillside Ramblings,* page 14: **Scota**; The fifth and final colony which inhabited Ireland called themselves various names at different periods in their history, Gaels, Milesians or at times, Scoti, from Scota, the Mother of the Milesius. In Irish legends Scota was said to be the daughter of an Egyptian Pharaoh named Cingris. Source: Thomas D'Arcy McGee, B.C.L., History of Ireland, Volume I, Cameron & Ferguson Edition, Glasgow, Scotland, 1855.

*Grainan of Aileach,* page 15: The **Grianan of Aileach** is a group of historic structures atop a 244 metre (801 ft) hill in County Donegal. The main structure is a stone ringfort, thought to have been built by the Uí Néill in the sixth or seventh century CE; although there is evidence that the site had been in use before the fort was built. It has been identified as the seat of the Kingdom of Aileach and one of the royal sites of Gaelic Ireland. **Taliesin**, or **Talisen**, was a 6th century early Brythonic poet of Sub-Roman Britain whose work has survived in a Middle Welsh manuscript, the Book of Taliesin. Taliesin was a renowned bard who is believed to have sung at the courts of at least three Brythonic kings. **Amergin** is a bard and judge for the Milesians in the Irish Mythological Cycle. He was appointed Chief Ollam of Ireland by his two brothers the kings of Ireland. A number of poems attributed to Amergin are part of the Milesian mythology.

*Love at First Sight,* page 18: **Brian Boru**, killed at Clontarf after he defeated the Danes in the 11th Century.

*Charity, Sweet Charity,* page 28: Halfpenny Bridge is a small walking bridge in the centre of Dublin.

*Ghosts by the Sea,* page 31: There are two **Tintern Abbeys**; the one in Wales made famous by Wordsworth's poem "Lines Written a Few Miles Above Tintern Abbey" and the one Ireland on the Hook Peninsula, County Wexford.

*Tribute to P. J. O'Hare,* page 34: Kevin J. Woods, *The Last Leprechauns of Ireland*, Original Writing Ltd., Dublin, Ireland, 2011--Details the story of P. J.'s meetings with the Leprechauns.

*Climbing Slieve Foy,* page 35: **Slieve Foy** is the highest peak of a ridge of mountains collectively referred to as Carlingford Mountain, which rises near the town of Carlingford, County Louth.

*Meeting Ghosts in Guildhall,* page 38: I always had an intuitive sense that somehow I was connected to Londonderry in Northern Ireland and even wrote about the city in a poem published in Cameos in 1985 long before I had traveled to Ireland. During my tour of Guildhall in 1990 I had the feeling that somehow I belonged but had no proof when I wrote this poem. In later trips to Derry with the help of historians

Brian Mitchell and Mickey McGuinness, I located my maternal Ellis and Best ancestors in the honour (tax) roles of Londonderry in 1690. As a result of this chance encounter I continued my research over the next few years; which resulted in the publication of the historical novel *The Hawthorn Bush* in 2005.

*Rosaleen,* page 44: **Crana Knits in Buncrana, Donegal** was supported by a small grant from the local government that subsidized a cross border development project that encouraged women on both sides of the northern border to knit sweaters for the Crana Woolen Mill. Owned and operated by Rosaleen Heagarty, Rosaleen tried very hard to keep the mill going during very difficult economic times. She saw how important the project was not only for the success of her business but also for the women who came into her shop once a week. They came in the beginning to discuss knitting but soon their gatherings became an outlet to discuss a war over which they had no control.

*Preparing for the Twelfth,* page 46: The correct name for the **City of Derry (Londonderry)** has changed many times since its early beginnings. For a first time visitor to the area, the use of a preferred name, either Derry or Londonderry, immediately indicates your political sympathies. So with caution and respect for both sides of my ancestral linage, Presbyterian and Catholic, North and South, I write both names and urge the reader to use whichever name feels "light" to you.

*Alive at Newgrange,* page 52: **Tír na nÓg** (Land of Youth) This spelling from Peter Berresford Ellis, *A Dictionary of Irish Mythology*, Constable and Company Limited, 10 Orange Street, London, UK, WC2H 7EG, 1987.

*Skating to Narva*, page 75: **Here where the fire burned** is a reference to the Second World War.

*Costume Ball,* page 95: Shortly after its construction, I visited the **Canadian Museum of Civilization**, the acclaimed symbol of our Canadian identity. Upon entering the Grand Hall, tears welled up within me and I gasped for breath at the sight of the Totem Poles and the Spirit of Haida Gwaii. Pride of country, its history and people overwhelmed me; "Yes, yes," I murmured to myself, "those who have designed and created this masterpiece of stone and steel have captured the essence of Canada." It was indeed a great surprise and a thrill when in a telephone conversation a number of years later I was invited to be a trustee of the same institution. I found myself working for the next four years with its leaders and board members from across the nation who were as proud as I to participate in such an important symbol of our Canadian identity. This pride was particularly evident during the construction and official opening of the Museum of War.
Unfortunately time and tide have brought other leaders and Board Members who have a different vision for this grand and glorious place, who have sought to change its name, and who wish to rewrite Canadian history. But it is my belief the land will rise up again, the Raven will

soar and the Spirit of Haidi Gwaii will return to our shores once again. The poem, *Costume Ball*, was written during the period when I was a Member of the Board of Trustees of the Canadian Museum of Civilization Corporation.

*Finding our Voice*, page 97: **CAIS** refers to Canadian Association for Irish Studies. CBC refers to Canadian Broadcasting Corporation. **Morningside** refers to the CBC three-hour morning radio programme that aired from 1976 until 1997. **Gzowski** refers to Peter Gzowski the host of Morningside from 1982 until 1997 during which time he and the show became much loved Canadian icons. **Dead Dog Café** refers to the CBC radio show, Dead Dog Café Comedy Hour in which Aboriginal actors offered up a mix of scathing political critique, social commentary, and mock cultural stereotyping. **Lewis** refers to Stephen Lewis, leader of the Ontario New Democratic Party for most of the 1970s. He was appointed Canada's ambassador to the United Nations in 1984 and subsequently worked in various international positions for the UN, including as special envoy for HIV/AIDS in Africa. He became known as an exemplary figure of Canadian humanitarianism. **Axworthy** refers to Lloyd Axworthy, a Liberal member of Parliament from 1983 to 2000, holding ministerial appointments in five different departments, ending as the Minster of Foreign Affairs. In that capacity he was instrumental in securing the Ottawa Treaty that bans land mines. He became a strong voice in the campaign against the use of child soldiers. **De Chastelain** refers to John de Chastelain, a Canadian military leader and diplomat. He was twice appointed to Chief of the Defence Staff. In 1995 he became active in the Northern Ireland peace process and was eventually instrumental in the disarmament of paramilitary groups.

*On Hearing of Brian Goodwin's Passing,* page 118: When I arrived at Schumacher College in Dartington, England in September 2001, the whole world was still reeling from the chaos of September 11th. I entered a room full of strangers speaking various languages when a kind gentleman approached introducing himself as a fellow Canadian. **Brian Goodwin** went on to tell me he spent his summers as a youth visiting grandparents at Baie Vert, New Brunswick. As our conversation progressed he confided in me that one of his ancestors was a young drummer who came to New Brunswick in the 1700's with the British and whose drum was still on display encased in glass at Fort Beasejour. I was pleased to be able to tell him I had seen the drum. Brian was my mentor during my stay at Schumacher College and his discussions on Gaia and Deep Ecology had a profound impact on my philosophical development.
**Brian Carey Goodwin** (25 March 1931 – 15 July 2009) was a Canadian mathematician and biologist, a Professor Emeritus at the Open University and a founder of the field of theoretical biology. He made key contributions to the foundations of biomathematics, complex systems and generative models in

developmental biology. He was one of the prominent scientists who suggested that a reductionist view of nature will fail to explain complex features. He is the author of *How the Leopard Changed Its Spots: The Evolution of Complexity*.

***Red Crane Against the Moon,*** page 121: Inspired by Shirley Bear's pencil drawing of Grandmother Moon.

# About the Author

Thelma Ann Brennan, B.A., M.A., is a gifted New Brunswick writer whose diverse body of work ranges from biography to historical novels to collections of poetry. Her publications include *The Real Klondike Kate* (1990, Goose Lane Editions), a nationally acclaimed biography of the Johnville NB native Katherine Ryan, who became a heroine of the North and made Canadian history as the first female member of the Northwest Mounted Police. *The Hawthorn Bush* (2005, Borealis Press) is a novel based on the author's ancestral heritage - both "orange and green" – and recounts the Irish contribution to the development of Canada. She has co-authored two collections of poetry, *Cameos* (1985, Henley Publishing) and *Feathers & Shells* (2000, Henley Publishing). She is also the author of an unpublished monograph, *Thinking Like a Mountain: The Philosophy of Arne Naess and the Deep Ecology Movement, 1972–2005*. Her work has appeared in the journals Cormorant, Canadian Women's Studies, Vox Feminarium, and in the book *Stories of My Neighbour's Faith: Narratives from World Religions in Canada*, edited by Susan L. Scott.

Ann Brennan is a founding member of the New Brunswick Writers Federation. She is also a member of Pen Canada, The Writers Union of Canada, and the Canadian Association of Irish Studies. She is a former participant in the New Brunswick's Writers in Schools Program, encouraging youth to discover their heritage through their own research and documentation of local history.

Recognized for her many contributions to the arts and cultural communities, Ann Brennan was appointed to the Board of Trustees of the Museum of Civilization in Ottawa soon after it was initiated. Committed to the enhancement of Canadian-Irish relations, she brought together 110 musicians, actors, and historians from both Northern Ireland and the Republic of Ireland for a three-week performing arts tour of New Brunswick in 1991. She led a similar exchange two years later in Northern Ireland in support of the Irish Peace Process. In 2004 she served as an election observer with the Canadian mission to Ukraine.

As a writer, Ann Brennan's work has taken her to Ireland where she was a guest lecturer at the Charles Macklin Autumn School in Culdaff, and to British Columbia and the Yukon for an anniversary Klondike Kate book tour. She has studied at Schumacher College in the UK and received a Master's degree in history from the University of New Brunswick in 2006.

Ann Brennan is the mother of six children, has eleven grandchildren, and one great-grandchild. She lives with her husband, Raymond, in the historic Irish settlement of Johnville, Carleton County New Brunswick. Her farm home overlooks the agricultural and forested landscape of the Saint John River Valley. She and her family are among the primary organizers of the Johnville Picnic, a community celebration that has been held continuously since the 1880s.

## About the Publisher

Chapel Street Editions publishes fine books on the natural history, human history, and cultural life of the Saint John River Region.

We are dedicated to publishing the work of writers and artists of our region, and to publishing books that advance an understanding of the relationship between the natural world, culture, and human adaptation to the environment.

We believe a vibrant cultural life rests on a strong attachment to place: This means a strong attachment to the land, the built environment, and the communities where we live.

For additional information visit
www.chapelstreeteditions.com

www.ingramcontent.com/pod-product-compliance
Ingram Content Group UK Ltd.
Pitfield, Milton Keynes, MK11 3LW, UK
UKHW042019190726
13854UKWH00005B/2365

9 780993 672521